20 Simple Real Estate Lead Generation Strategies

20 Simple Real Estate Lead Generation Strategies

The Life Blood of YOUR Business

Midas Franklin

To order additional copies of this book, contact:
Xlibris Corporation
1-888-795-4274
www.Xlibris.com
Orders@Xlibris.com
51203

CONTENTS

ABOUT THE AUTHOR

MIDAS FRANKLIN

Let me introduce myself, my name is Midas and I'm an entrepreneur, author, and real estate investor. More importantly than that I'm a father and a husband, and I'm a strong believer in the value of family. In April of 2012 my lovely wife and I celebrated 28 wonderful years together. I'm also the proud father of 9 children (6 daughters and 3 sons. Yes, I am truly blessed beyond my wildest dreams). My family is the reason I get up every morning. They give my life purpose. I wish to thank them here and now for their inspiration and support, without which none of this would've been possible and I would not be the person I am today.

I started my career some 30 years ago and have been engaged in the real estate industry in a number of different capacities over the years, from contracting to investor. I've experienced much: ups, downs, even sideways movement in the real estate market, yet I can say without reservation that real estate has always both challenged and inspired me. You see . . . Real Estate investing, if done right, is a business of helping people and that is perhaps the most gratifying aspect of it, and as long as helping people is the foremost consideration in your business the rewards will be immeasurable.

So after surveying my experiences over these last 30 years or so in the real estate industry I felt it was time for me to write this book. This book expresses my business philosophy, while listing the sources, strategies, and techniques I use in my business to get customers. Hopefully you will find this book a good read. I certainly have intended it that way. I hope it will help as many people as possible to experience the same wonderful lifestyle real estate investing can bring.

Oh, and BTW please feel free to pass along any comments or suggestions you might have, I'd love to hear from you. mailto:midas@ newworldreinvesting.com

Thank you and I hope you enjoy the book.

CHAPTER 1

FUNDAMENTALS OF A SUCCESSFUL REAL ESTATE INVESTING BUSINESS

The real estate business has always been a popular career choice among entrepreneurs. It has brought fortunes to many leading business icons. Before the recent hit of recession on the global economy in the year 2008, the real estate sector was in a boom phase in which the industry generated huge profits for people who prudently invested in property ventures.

Most people today are probably thinking that after the recent economic turmoil it would be foolish to invest money in real estate. If you are among them, than I am here to challenge your perspective on that perception! Real estate to me has never been a rotten egg. It is one of the very few industries which are usually characterized by rising prices, although not all markets are on the rise at the same time. Some markets can be stagnant or even falling while other local and the overall national market are on an upswing.

The last few decades prior to the recession witnessed unprecedented steep high gains in the prices of real estate, yet since then the opposite is true, but no matter which way the market is trending, up or down, over the long run real estate values usually increase, profits can be made, and prudent investments are the key to success, not only in the real estate investing business but in any industry anywhere around the world. If you want to be successful, all you need is information and the ability to conduct prudent critical decision making.

Now the question is how to ensure prudence in your decision making. In order to make intelligent decisions it is especially important to comprehend the essential fundamentals of the real estate investing business. This whole text is hence designed to guide you on how to make profits with your real estate business and to examine the tactics and strategies of a successful real estate investing business. But before diving into that further first let's define what constitutes an actual real estate investing business!

Real Estate Investing Business:

The term Real Estate refers to properties such as land and buildings. It basically encompasses lands along with improvements to the land such as buildings, wells, fences and other site improvements and can also be commonly referred to as the real properties.

Real estate investments are essentially investments in such immovable properties. Hence, the term real estate investment (or what is known commonly as property investment) simply means investment in any real property usually in the form of a purchase of that property with the intention of generating positive returns on your investment or simply gaining profits out of the deal by selling the property at some future time.

The range of properties that an investor can hold includes apartments, plots, condominiums, town houses, duplexes, bungalows, buildings, commercial properties and even vacant land.

Types of Real Estate Investments:

With the development of private property ownership in prominent countries of the world, the real estate business has become a major sector of the economy in those countries. Buying and selling of real estate soon thereafter developed into the concrete enterprise that we usually today refer to as the *Real Estate Industry*.

The people that represent buyers and sellers in real estate dealings are commonly referred to as real estate brokers or agents, others who are involved in the buying and selling of a property are closing agents, appraisers, and property inspectors.

With changing times the real estate industry has expanded widely and real estate transactions have taken many forms.

The real estate investor has basically 'interest in land'
Ian Woychuk

The *interest* can usually be categorized into two common forms. The first is the 'ownership interest', where the investors have full rights over the ownership of the land or property i.e. they have the legal title of the land or property and hence also assumes the associated risks. The other type of *interest* is the leasehold where interest only exists when a landowner agrees to pass some of their rights on to a tenant in exchange for a payment of rent. If you rent an apartment, you have a leasehold interest in real estate[1].

Building upon these two fundamental concepts, real estate investments can be categorized into the following basic types:

- Property Flipping
- Fix and Flip
- Properties for rental
- REIT

Property Flipping:

Property flipping is direct buying and selling. This is one of the most common forms of real estate business and works well when the prices in the market are soaring, where investors purchase a property and straight away put it for sale, to generate profits because of rising prices. Another form of flipping known as *Wholesaling* works for distressed properties needing significant repairs that can be purchased at a steep discount and then flipped to a Rehabber (Fix & Flip—described in the next paragraph).

Fix and Flip:

Fix and flip is similar to flipping. The only difference is that after buying a property the investors do some renovations and then put the property on sale (they fix and then flip) to secure more profits. Again this works well when the prices are rising.

Properties for rental:

Investing in rental properties is another real estate business avenue. It is also one of the most commonly used methods, where the investor purchases a property, finds a renter and rents it out for a fixed amount of monthly rental. The landlord is the real owner of the property hence all expenses on the property lies on the landlord plus any increases in the property rates are also the landlord's rights.

REIT:

Apart from the above mentioned types there are numerous other ways to invest in the real estate industry for profits. For example investing in shares of "Real Estate Investment Trusts (REIT)", these are effective when you either lack enough capital for individual investments or you lack expertise. REIT and other such groups are basically companies that invest in the real estate and then issue shares in exchange.

These are just a few common types of investments that take place in a real estate market. Now let's explore the basic fundamentals of a real estate investing business.

Fundamentals of a Real Estate Investing Business:

Apart from the above mentioned basic forms, real estate investing can take on various other identities which we will explore throughout this text, but one thing that underlines the whole of any real estate business is the *Lead Flow*. As a real estate investor you need to have buyers and sellers available to you all the time. *Lead Flow* is the heart of any real estate investing business. In order to become successful in real estate and gain positive returns on your investments, it is essential that you know the three basic fundamentals of maintaining your lead flow for your real estate business. These fundamentals are listed below:

Lead Generation	**Attracting and finding buyer and seller leads**
Lead Management	**Organizing and maintaining the leads**
Lead Leveraging	**Making the most from your leads.**

Lead generation and effective lead management is the core element behind the success of any real estate investing business. Irrespective of its form or type, leveraging the best performance out of your leads is the ultimate tool for creating wealth. This is why we have dedicated this entire text to help you explore the insights of this business and to help you learn tactics and strategies on how to effectively generate leads, what are the sources of obtaining buyers and sellers from both offline and online sources, how to ensure positive cash generation in this business, etc.—hence this information will help you become the successful real estate empire builder which you simply could not be without the benefit of the information in this book.

CHAPTER 2

EFFECTIVE REAL ESTATE LEAD GENERATION STRATEGIES

The single most important thing behind the success of any business is its leads i.e. the prospective buyers, customers or users of a company's products or service. The same is true for the real estate industry. Developing and maintaining effective buyer's leads is the surest path to success. No buyers or leads simply mean—*NO SALES!*

Now let's be more specific. When we talk specifically about the real estate business, things are a bit tougher. The reason behind this is the need to seek effective sellers at the right time as well. Yes, in order to carry on this business profitably the real estate investor does not only need to look for the buyers of the properties but at the same time they have to constantly attract lucrative deals from sellers also. This makes the business more tactical. But this should not cause you any worry, as we will explore in this text various ways in which you can generate effective leads from both sides of the business, which in turn will, if properly implemented, in the end raise your bottom line.

Two Broad Categories of the Lead Generation Methods

Before disclosing a number of lead generation strategies, it is important to highlight the two broad categories of the lead generation methods.

- Offline Methods
- Online Methods

- **Offline Methods:**

Offline methods of lead generation usually comprise the traditional ways of real estate lead generation. These methods are often physical in nature including offline contact, face to face meetings, direct advertising, referrals, business cards etc. All of these will be discussed in detail later in our text. The offline methods are usually regarded as more effective in terms of turning your buyers and sellers leads into prospective clients. However, it limits your reach to your prospects as compared to the online methods discussed below.

- **Online Methods:**

Since the advent of the internet and the World Wide Web the outreach of anyone is now global and has been expanded near infinitely. Hence, it has become evident for businesses to enter into the online arena. The same is also true for a real estate business. Online presence is also becoming the most effective source of generating leads for businesses. Online methods of lead generation range from website marketing, SEO based marketing, e-newsletters, e-mail marketing and many other techniques. These methods and tactics and their effectiveness will also be discussed later in detail in this text.

Now the question is how a real estate investor can optimize their lead generation. Regardless of the methods you use there are a number of strategies that can help you to optimize your lead generation process. But in order to get the most out of your lead generation strategies it is vital to comprehend the essential steps involved in the lead generation process.

The Lead Generation Process:

For every real estate investor it is essential to understand that lead generation is not a small task to undertake. Many investors never realize the importance of this process. Lead generation is in fact *the* core business activity and requires constant testing and tweaking. It should be planned and carried out as a long-term income generating business strategy.

According to a research report on *'what really works in lead generation'* posted by the Keller Center, it was concluded after a survey of a large group of over 50,000 Real Estate Professionals from North America that effective lead generation involves three basic steps:

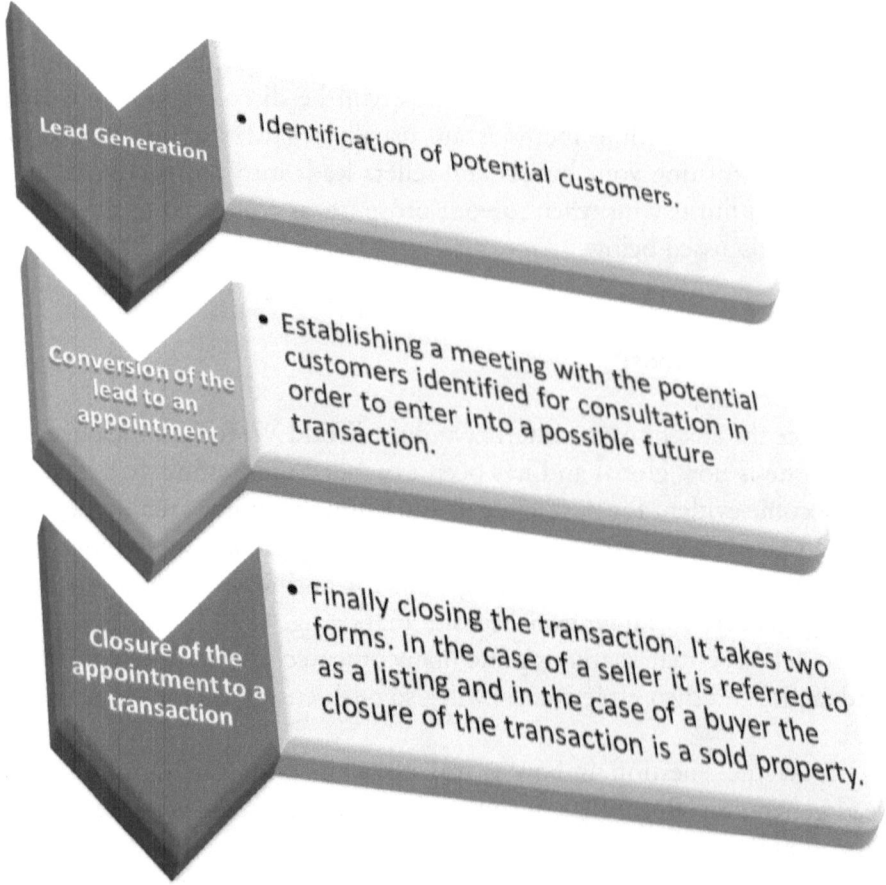

Lead Generation
- Identification of potential customers.

Conversion of the lead to an appointment
- Establishing a meeting with the potential customers identified for consultation in order to enter into a possible future transaction.

Closure of the appointment to a transaction
- Finally closing the transaction. It takes two forms. In the case of a seller it is referred to as a listing and in the case of a buyer the closure of the transaction is a sold property.

Effective Lead Generation Strategies:

Now let's come to the real debate. How professional real estate investors maximize the productivity of the lead generation process? Listed below are a few successful strategies:

- **Differentiation:**

  Differentiation is as important in a real estate business as it is for any other business, especially in the era of information technology where customers are bombarded on a daily basis with thousands of ads. Offline and online sources of marketing are enormous and are an effective means of communication and lead synthesis. Hence in order to attract people towards your business it is critical to have marketing campaigns that are innovative enough to stay in the forefront of the minds of potential customers and compelling enough to move them to action to ultimately do business with you.

In a real estate setting your message should be benefit-driven enough to demand the attention of your target leads.

- **Copywriting:**

Your message should be clear and complete to drive attention. Copywriting is therefore one of the most important but often ignored areas of a good marketing campaign in a real estate business.

A talented copywriter basically brings your story to life with the magic of their words, imagery, and phrase. Effective copywriting phrases the contents in such a way that it gets the reader attracted towards your business and leads them to get in touch with you for further information

Unfortunately, many investors completely ignore the importance of this element and hence experience failure in their marketing campaigns, if the lead cannot glean a clear message from what they read they are much less likely to contact you for further information.

- **Faster lead follow-up:**

Many real estate investors successfully generate hundreds of buyer and seller leads but it is observed that even then they cannot generate sales or business. Their lead conversion rate is extremely low. Why does this happen? One of the main reasons for this, out of the many possible causes, is they don't follow-up their leads. It is especially important to follow-up your leads so that they don't get off-track. Faster lead follow-up to initial buyer or seller inquiries can keep your leads away from other competitors. In the Three-Stage Model article reviewed in the Research Insider—*Marketing Mix* it was observed that faster follow-up to initial lead inquiries resulted in higher conversion rates. The research was basically initiated to examine the relationship between time to follow-up and conversion rates in the real estate industry. The results are indicated by the following graph which shows that the business leads that were followed-up within five days of being identified showed 20% higher rates of conversion to sales than those that wait longer than seven to ten days for a sales visit[2].

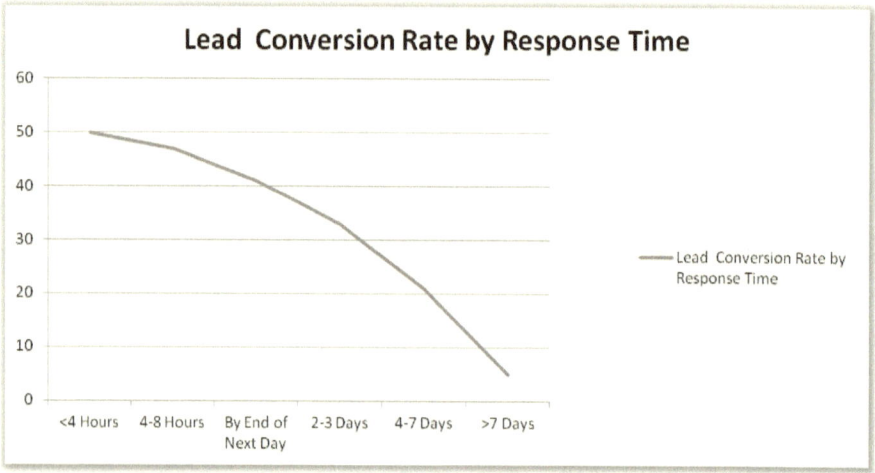

- **Professional expertise for closure:**

  Lead closure is the most technical step of the process and requires exceptional expertise on the part of the marketer. When your leads have been identified, marketed to and followed-up with, you now require a qualified salesperson to close the deal. Without proper closing techniques real estate investors may lose the momentum of their campaign.

- **Follow past customers for future referrals:**

  Referrals are the most important and effective source of generating future business leads. Every real estate investor must understand that the ultimate goal of the lead generation campaign should be not only identifying leads and turning them into customers, but also to turn those customers into advocates for your product or service.

You can also expand your networking to get referrals for your business. This aspect is so important that we have allocated a whole chapter in this text for this topic. Later in the text we will explore referrals and its importance in more detail and explore the tactics to generate referrals for your business.

The above strategies if followed properly can maximize the efficacy of your lead generation campaign and help you achieve your ultimate goal of building a successful real estate business.

CHAPTER 3

REAL ESTATE LEAD GENERATION

In the previous chapter we explored the lead generation process, its methods and effective strategies designed to optimize your lead generation scheme. So what's new in this chapter . . . . ! Scroll down and find out!

By now, you have hopefully understood very well that lead generation is *the* core element behind the success of any real estate investment business. An effective lead generating process involves finding and reaching prospective buyers and sellers of properties well ahead of your competition in this fiercely competitive real estate market.

But our base line is finding or locating *targeted* leads. Many real estate investors do realize the importance of lead generation but what they don't know is how to get to the buyer and seller leads? What should property investors do to get to their target market? This chapter is dedicated to assisting you in exploring various effective tactics or tools that will help you to reach and attract your target leads.

Effective lead generation tactics

As mentioned previously, buyer and seller leads are the life blood that keep your business alive in the real estate market, hence the process should be effective and ongoing. Traditionally most leads were generated through buying lead lists and calling those people to secure business. But today real estate lead generation goes way beyond cold calls (cold calls are where you as investors would contact unknown people by phone or door knocking to market your business). It is considered by many to be a complete waste of time today. But why is this so? It is because when you buy the *leads* you are actually calling people who are not familiar with you. They do not know anything about your background or reputation. As buying, selling and/or renting a property are considered to be major decisions in a person's life, it requires investors to develop more personalized relationships to reach their leads. With cold calling you are taking the risk of being turned down as many people do not appreciate calls of that kind; hence cold calling is not a recommended method of finding leads in this day and age.

So what is the best way to get leads then? The best alternative is to let people know about your services and then make people want to come to you. That sounds great doesn't it?

Now you must be asking yourself "just how can I make this happen for my business?" Well here are some proven tactics for you:

- **Direct mailing:**

     One of the most common forms of lead generation is direct mailing. Direct mail campaigns really work. The only problem is they require relatively large sums of money to begin mailing potential leads and this is more difficult when you are new in the business. But these campaigns can get people to call you. The reasons they are effective are two-fold as firstly you can reach the people who are actually looking to buy or sell some real estate property and secondly they call you themselves.

     A survey conducted by a group of researchers on a number of real estate professionals detailing their total spending on various lead generation methods, the results of which are displayed on the graph below, shows the spending allocations on the top nine areas.

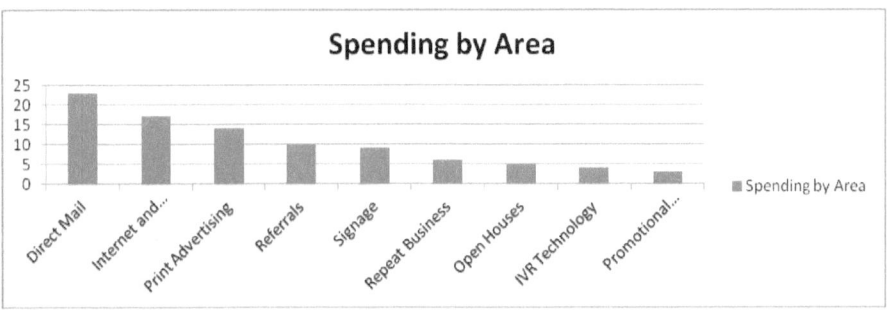

According to the survey it was concluded that out of eighteen lead building methods, direct mailing is the one in which on average real estate professionals dedicate the highest amount of spending[3].

Hence this highlights the significance of direct mailing in generating real estate leads.

- **Improve networking:**

    The world has become a global village. Today's era of information technology and advance sources of e-communication has brought a revolution in the business world. Real estate investors can take advantage of these sources to improve their contacts and enhance networking.

    Networking is a proven way to let people know about your business and your services. Especially in the real estate investing business networking is viewed as the best marketing strategy to build value and trust in the minds of your prospects, and hence get you effective leads. Expanding your contacts by getting in touch with various housing contractors, local mortgage brokers, real estate attorneys, developers and even with your family and friends can increase your chances of them passing your name to their clients and their acquaintances. Traditionally, effective means of networking were attending various networking events; cocktail parties, family gatherings, conventions, home shows, etc. which are still regarded as effective tactics to generate leads.

    Apart from them the most significant sources of networking in modern times are of course the social websites like Facebook, Twitter, etc. that can help expand your business enormously. In the up-coming chapters we will discuss in detail about the importance and ways of generating real estate leads through social media marketing.

- **Promote On line presence:**

    Developing and maintaining a website is another smart way of generating business leads as a majority of prospects begin their real estate searches on the internet. It is a valuable way of staying in contact with your clients, 24 hours a day. Online marketing and Search Engine Optimization (SEO) focused techniques can help you increase your online visibility and enhances your chances of generating effective leads. In the next chapter we will explore how you can effectively employ online lead generation techniques.

- **Use testimonials:**

  Testimonials or endorsements from your past clients are one of the best sources of generating effective future leads. Referrals from past customers can help you get genuine leads and help you build your reputation.

- **Set-up incentive programs:**

  You can setup various monetary and non-monetary incentive programs to pursue people and gain more potential leads. Referral incentive programs can encourage people to bring prospective customers to your business. For example incentives can be in the form of a gift, a free product such as a report or newsletter membership, or as just mentioned, can be monetary in nature.

Lead Generation is a continuous process. It is not something that is done once. In fact, it needs to happen consistently to ensure that you continue securing future business for the long term health and wealth of your company. And the above tactics will most definitely assist you in your lead search (as well as helping you in thrashing your competitors).

CHAPTER 4

ONLINE LEAD GENERATION TECHNIQUES

Today many businesses are vying for online space and seek to adopt web marketing strategies to increase their business leads, which in turn should enhance their sales, and eventually increase their profits. According to a report published by Price Water House Coopers (PWC), in the United States, U.S. $16.5 billion were expected to be spent on online marketing in the year 2006[4]. *Hence with more than eighty percent* of buyers and sellers using the internet today, it is essential for the real estate investor to use online methods for generating buyer and seller leads, as most of these buyers and sellers go online to do their own research looking for specific information. People today want to gather more and more information and want access to professional real estate tools before signing up the services of an agent or investor. So why shouldn't you be the one that they end up working with?

Here are some online techniques to achieve your objective:

Effective Online Lead Generation Techniques

- **Use of Websites:**

  As mentioned earlier using your own website is the most effective and cost efficient way to stay in contact with your clients 24 hours a day and to get you a list of prospective leads. An attractive and informative website can help you develop your own list of leads by harvesting the details of the traffic that visit your website. You can do this by simply asking them to check a box and enter their name or email address. Interested leads will surely enter their personal data to receive additional information. Hence, this will help you generate your own list of leads. You can also add testimonials to grab your prospects attention. Also there are various websites that use "squeeze pages" which compel their visitors to provide their email IDs in order to access the website. This could also help generate leads.

- **Article Marketing:**

Posting articles related to the real estate industry at various online sources can also generate leads. Firstly, because a topical article will attract a person who is obviously interested in the topic in question and willing to actively seek out information about it on the Internet. Secondly, well developed content can show your level of expertise and knowledge. Thirdly, it is not a direct sales campaign, so there are fewer chances of your leads ignoring it. Also by linking your articles to your web sites you can help attract web traffic towards your site and increase your leads.

- **E-Newsletters:**

Another source of online marketing in demand today is the e-newsletter. Through effective newsletters you can provide informative articles and show your level of expertise to your leads. An e-newsletter is also more effective than a direct sales letter as most real estate leads usually hate direct promotions.

- **E-mail Marketing:**

E-mail marketing is also a cheaper way of reaching hundreds of leads worldwide and can be used with other marketing tools.

- **Corporate Blogs:**

Posting regular updates on corporate blogs are essential for building public relations and help you expand your circle. These blogs can get you effective and reliable leads.

- **Social Media Sites:**

  Famous social media sites like Facebook, Twitter, and LinkedIn are also a powerful source of lead generation and will help you improve your business. These constitute the latest lead generation techniques and will be discussed further in detail later in the text.

- **Use Online Forums to Get Free Leads:**

  One way to develop an effective list of leads is the use of forums. Try to join forums that are not only active and highly responsive, but are related to your field and can help you get future business leads. These techniques are referred to as soft marketing techniques that help you gain prospective customers trust and then you can market your offerings directly to them by collecting email addresses of the people who are interested in your product or service(s).

- **Using online form builder:**

  Online form builder can help you generate leads. A good online lead generation form can get you information about your leads, so that you can turn them into potential customers while building relationships.

All these techniques can generate you effective leads of buyers and sellers, but you should remember the following:

- **Determine your customer's interest first.**

- **Develop attractive and effective content.**

- **Your articles should be SEO focused as 81% of internet users find websites by using search engines.**

- **Use back links etc.**

The above tactics are just a few of the many ways that can help you generate business leads effectively online.

CHAPTER 5

TOP REASONS TO USE ONLINE TOOLS

Business has always gained new business through traditional lead generation techniques. Especially in businesses like real estate investing where people often assume that face to face or physical marketing is the only key to success. So why have we been discussing online lead generation techniques?

Let's take you through some of the advantages of online methods of lead generation.

- As mentioned previously today more than eighty percent of people use the internet for their information search. So if you want good leads, you need to go online to keep pace with changing life styles.
- Generating your leads on social media websites can bring two fold profits for you. Firstly, it can reach to masses without any geographical boundaries. According to research statistics nearly two thirds of the world's internet population now visits a *social network* or *blog* site weekly[5]. Secondly, it helps you generate and spread referrals to other people or networks or what is commonly known as word-of-mouth marketing. A latest study from Pew Internet highlights that social networks are becoming a popular source of information and almost 89% of people forward news, events, and vendor specific information to people in their network[6.]
- Online lead generation techniques are deemed as more effective than traditional approaches like cold calling or telemarketing as it helps your clients to get to you rather than you going to them. For example if you just post industry related articles (SEO focused) on various directories, blogs, or online forums regularly and then link

it to your websites, your leads will come to you. The leads who are interested search and reach you directly. This will generate effective leads for you and you can then customize your services to your leads according to their search queries.

- Online search helps you build your repute in the industry. Emailed searches allow the real estate investor to send a comprehensive list of properties on the market customized to the specification and research objectives of every particular user who signs up for their services. This will allow the investor to promote their best portfolio, aiding to the branding of themselves as an industry expert.

- Cost efficiency is another important factor that online sources offer. In fact online lead generating techniques are one of the lowest cost techniques as compared to offline means of marketing. At the same time it provides you higher reach as well.

- Online lead generation techniques are preferred by your clients. As many people today prefer investors not calling them for marketing. Instead they seek information themselves online. That is why websites and online promotions work for them.

- Online tools also provide an avenue for greater customer service. For example if you post a free comparative analysis tool on your site, where your viewers can compare prices of the properties of their interest and specifications, you have already done your work. Your potential clients cannot only make quick decisions but they also brand you as trustworthy, efficient and an expert investor and will definitely approach you for more information or to enter into a transaction with you.

Hence online sources provide you low-cost and highly effective lead generation solutions and are helpful in assisting you to create lasting impressions and strong connections with your prospective customers.

CHAPTER 6

LAWS OF ONLINE LEAD GENERATION

By now you must have realized the benefits of online lead generation techniques. Most of you I'm sure are already implementing all of these lead generation techniques to boost the number of your leads and better your business. But have you generated *"effective leads"* successfully? If not, then you must be wandering about what has gone wrong with your methods? This chapter will surely provide you with some answers to that question.

Instead of all those expected enormous benefits from online lead generation techniques sometimes you don't see the desired results. So here in this chapter we will explore a few basic laws of online lead generation that you must follow and stick to in order to experience a successful marketing campaign. Regardless of the lead generation technique or method you use online, you must adhere to these laws if you want to make your lead generation campaign work.

Laws of Online Lead Generation

Here are a few basic laws:

Law # 1: Web traffic is not necessarily equal to *"effective"* leads:

Most of you whose online lead generation campaign has failed, must have observed that even after making an attractive website with the latest tools and techniques, or even posting regular informative articles on related forums, online directories, or blogs you are unable to generate a sale or close any transactions. Even if you attract enormous numbers of web visitors to your site you still generate no sales. Why is this so?

Let's understand this with a simple example. Just imagine that you have an attractive corner juice shop or fresh fruit juice stall in an extensively flooded location, where a huge number of shoppers and street foot traffic passes by daily. Everyone sees your stall but no one stops or actually buys juice. Will you be happy or content with that? Of course not! Your ultimate purpose will be to actually sell juice. The same is true for the real estate marketers. Many attract web traffic to their sites but fail to close sales. This happens when marketers view web traffic as their leads. But traffic is not leads.

As a real estate marketer your need is to generate leads out of your web visitors. You need to 'convert your traffic into your leads'. Once you have piqued the interest in your customer, it is now time to obtain their information. The prospect will now easily produce his or her contact information and get subscribed to your website and hence you can get a reliable and genuine lead for your business.

Now the dilemma is how will you do that? Here are a few techniques:

- **Add a Squeeze Page:** Many marketers add squeeze pages to their websites which compels visitors to provide their email IDs in order to access the website. It is a simple subscription form and asks the visitor to either sign up to get on the email list, or leave the website. This is a kind of *"forced lead"* that online lead generators use to build their list. The visitor has to make a choice here. This technique actually provides you with people who are seriously interested in your offering and this is precisely what a marketer should be striving for, a prospective lead. In order to add a squeeze page you can use many programs available online particularly for squeeze page creation.

- **Use Popup windows:** Pop-up windows are another way of generating information about your web visitor. Although mostly annoying, creating pop-up opt-in forms can get you effective leads. Pop-up windows can be triggered on entry or exit times, but use tactics to ensure it doesn't appear repeatedly once a person has already seen your pop-up.

- **Use an Auto Responder:** Auto responders are used by a number of companies today to build a list of leads. Whenever a web visitor tries to seek any further information online, auto responders could be used there that asks the visitor to furnish their name and email address in order to access that additional information. Again it gets you to people who are interested in what you are selling—real estate, rather than to complete strangers interested only in shopping for cookware, sports apparel, or pet care items.
  There are a number of very good and reasonably priced auto responder companies you can use, one of my favorites is AWeber, you can sign up by going here: http://www.aweber. com/?391375.

- **Opt-in email marketing:** Opt-in email marketing is another valuable approach to generating a profitable list. This also helps you to decrease the number of spam complaints as your prospects must confirm the request to subscribe to your email list.

All of these tactics actually call your web visitors for an action and help you generate effective leads through which you can directly get in touch with them and target them for a possible transaction.

Law # 2: Be valuable:

The first rule will only work if you stick to this rule too, as the web visitor will only leave their information or contact details for you, once they find you valuable and better than your competitors. Remember that

---

'Value and response are directly proportional'

The visitor of your website will remain anonymous until you present something useful and valuable in exchange for their action. Focus on developing a win-win relationship. Remember response goes up in proportion to the value of your offer.

Let's explore how you can do that:

- **Provide them the information they are interested in:** You must evaluate your customer. *Dig out* their needs. Build trust and generate your lead's interest by providing them a solution to their need or problem. Solve problems for your customers to make their lives easier.

- **Focus on content:** Make sure your content is good, interesting and informative. Research extensively the market trends affecting the housing and the real estate property sector. Don't make fake claims. Provide factual and up-to-date information. Put your efforts in your work and reap the profits.

> "What is written without effort is usually read without pleasure"[7]
>
> Samuel Johnson, a famous British Author

- **Avoid direct sales push:** Don't follow a push strategy, instead establish the fact that you do have expertise. Offer your visitors something that helps get customers to trust you, for example property listing updates to home shoppers. This will lead them to sign up with you.

Law# 3: Never forget to follow-up with your prospects:

Lead follow-up keeps your leads alive. Remember that real estate transactions are long term decisions that involve a good amount of investment. People will not generally convert into sales directly upon their first contact with you. It requires you to follow them up and keep visiting them regularly otherwise you will lose your prospective client, most likely to your competition that follows the strategies as listed above.

Hence, always remember that website traffic is only that—website traffic—unless you act upon it. You need to create leads by following these simple steps which will ultimately lead to your building of a prosperous business.

CHAPTER 7

OFFLINE LEAD GENERATION TECHNIQUES

Every real estate investor needs to generate more and more leads, until now our exploration has focused mainly on the online methods of lead generation, now let's explore some offline modes.

Cold Calling: Cold calling is one of the most traditional methods of generating leads. Many local investors just buy lead lists from some information source provider or lead building companies and start calling those people to market to them. Although, cold calling is one of the oldest and most common forms of lead generation, for most investors this method is not very effective. The call drop rate is very high. In fact if not handled properly it may even lose you a prospective lead as many people today don't like to be called for direct marketing. This particular method requires a specific type of approach and a high degree of expertise and experience.

- **Warm calling:** Warm calling is what I call a sophisticated conversion of cold calling. Rather than phoning people up and marketing them to sign up with your business, you can indirectly do this by inviting them to attend seminars or home shows etc. Interested people would surely respond to it positively and once they turn up at the event you can target them and market your business to them at this time.

- **Media Marketing:** Media marketing can be a great lead generation tool; however it turns out to be rather costly though. Advertising on TV and the radio can bring you leads but the costs should be matched with the associated benefits first.

- **Video Marketing:** You can develop your own CD-ROM or Video brochures to attract your leads but again this can also incur you huge costs if you are not doing it yourself.

- **Advertising in Print Media:** Advertising your services in local newspapers and magazines can be effective enough to generate leads, and can be relatively less expensive than video marketing.

- **Start Your Own Newsletter:** Starting a newsletter and getting people to sign up for it is another effective method of generating leads. But remember to give factual, up-to date and user-friendly information that is beneficial for your readers and develops your expertise in the minds of your prospects. Keep in mind that it requires adequate time, research, and money, but it can help you get positive leads. Also if your newsletter gets popular among your target market than you can make it even more lucrative by earning additional income from advertising revenue.

- **Write for Local Papers and Magazines:** You can even write for local newspapers or magazines and gain popularity. Article writing in newspapers can help you brand yourself as an expert in the industry and at the same time can bring you leads.

- **Business Cards:** Everyone prints business cards but the magic lies in where you supply them. You must give them to anyone you know and make sure that people disseminate them on your behalf.

- **Host a Seminar:** You can host a seminar on various topics such as how to get a home mortgage, how to buy a house, how to find a contractor etc. Everybody likes free information, and people would be delighted enough to get the information they need. If you provide them better ideas they remember you and if you effectively follow-up with them, they will be brilliant sources of real estate leads.

- **Guest Speaker:** If you can't host a seminar, volunteer yourself as a guest speaker at several local events and occasions at schools, day cares, colleges and various other seminar venues. It will provide you a chance to popularize yourself and can help you garner some additional leads.

These are a few of the many ways through which you can generate leads offline. Remember, the success of all these methods lies in networking. Every real estate investor should do everything they can possibly do to expand their network. In the upcoming chapters we will discuss various ways through which you can expand your contacts to get more prospective leads.

CHAPTER 8

LEAD GENERATION
THROUGH REFERRALS

In one of our previous chapters we had highlighted that referrals are one of the most effective lead generation strategies. Now let's explore here in detail what you can do to get more leads through referrals.

Lead Generation through Referrals

It's a well-accepted fact that every business should capitalize on its assets in order to get the maximum benefits out of them. In a factory the most valuable asset could be the machinery, similarly in the service industry the most valuable assets are the human resources.

Companies that invest in their assets will maximize their profits. Now, while talking about the real estate business what do you think is its most valuable asset? Well, if you ask me, I would say "the referrals". Referrals are the life blood of a real estate business. According to a survey of a group of professional real estate agents investigating what lead generation activities are most productive in generating leads in the real estate industry, it was observed that referrals are the most valuable and effective sources of lead generation. The graph below shows that lead generation through referrals was ranked highest among the various top lead generation sources evaluated in the survey[8].

Most Productive Areas

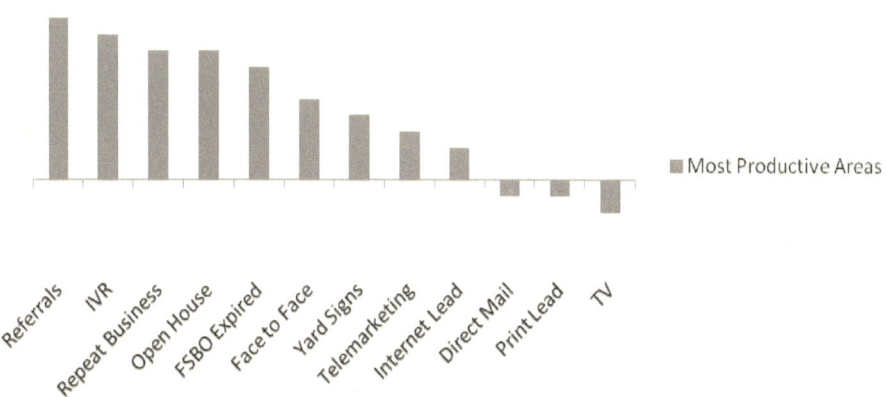

Many investors do realize the importance of referrals but the pity is they believe that referrals aren't generated, they just happen. This is a common marketing myth. As referrals are recommendations from your past customers telling another person about your products and services, most businesses assume that referrals are random events and cannot be generated. However, I totally disagree with that. In fact prudent marketers today incorporate an effective referral generating strategy to obtain positive leads or business prospects. Here are a few tips for you to activate an effective referral strategy:

- **Best satisfy your clients:** As referrals are recommendations from your clients about your service you must always ensure that you satisfy your client at your best. A well served client will market your services and prove to be a positive lead generator for you without you making more efforts.

- **Keep in touch with your clients:** If you want your clients to talk about you, you should ensure you stay alive in their minds. Keep sending those greeting cards, newsletters, etc. so that they don't forget you.

- **Provide Referral Based incentives:** You can often offer free coupons or commissions to your clients for every lead they generate for you.

- **Get them on your websites:** If your clients allow you, you can even ask them in a video interview how they find your services and post the video on your website.

- **Expand your networks:** Referrals don't necessarily come just from a satisfied client. You can even use your friends, relatives, and people from the industry, for example builders and brokers or property valuators, for referrals. They are often termed as warm leads to your business but they can still have the same positive effect on your lead generation efforts.

These tips can help you incorporate a proactive referral based strategy for lead generation and can help you gather *"effective leads"* for your business.

CHAPTER 9

ARE TRADITIONAL METHODS SUCCESSFUL OR NOT?

Having revealed most of the traditional and non-traditional methods of lead generation in the real estate industry, let's now discuss whether the traditional methods are successful today or not.

If you ask me, I would say that the success of any lead generation method depends on too many factors to make blanket evaluations of their effectiveness. For example factors such as the tactics used to grab leads, the follow-up rates, your service quality, the type of market, your particular skill set, attitude, & abilities, etc. With such a long list of diverse and subjective factors it seems to me it is rather unfair or illogical to state directly which methods are successful and which ones are not. It really depends more I think on how they are implemented.

The advocates of the latest advanced methods view various traditional methods such as cold calling, knocking doors, direct mailing, and printing ads in print media etc. as a complete waste of their efforts. They believe that there are better methods available today which are not only more productive but are more cost effective as well. Also they believe that many traditional methods are incapable of generating a robust response. Their opinion is that "a marketer has basically to wait for months to get a lead—finally!" using some traditional methods. Regrettably most traditional methods are slow to reveal results, expensive, and time consuming.

Additionally, considering that recent innovations in internet technology, mobile inventions, and the expansion & popularity of various social networking websites are low costs options of lead generation and marketing, comparisons can be even more difficult. These mediums have a huge reach globally and you can market yourself within seconds all over the world. And the best part is without investing much money. Also you can get a robust lead tracking mechanism with the latest feedback and follow-up techniques and hence, they believe, raise your chances of landing a customer.

Yet, after reviewing the latest market trends and statistics, few people rate traditional methods of lead generation as out-of date tactics that do not work in the prevailing market environment either. Especially considering that real estate markets for the most part are "local" in nature and therefore more congruent with the face-to-face let's shake hands kind of practices of the more traditional business model.

Now let's reveal the other side of the story. Just consider yourself as owner of a property wishing to sell it and visualize the scenario in which you live today. You might find an influx of *"house for sale"* or *"we buy houses"* sign boards all along the road. With so many contact details that eventually confuse you in deciding who to approach. And if you land on the internet, the situation will even get worse. You can get an endless list of real estate investors. Also once you click a site on the internet for gathering information, your own information is instantly put up for sale and you will soon find yourself inundated with investor inquiries. Just imagine, can you decide which one to contact? Now if in such a situation, you get contacted by an investor either through a phone call or a door knock (cold calling), listening to your queries directly and providing you solutions. Wouldn't you approach them? Hence to get out of the crowd of competitors and to get rid of the prospect's objections list; many investors now are converting back to the traditional methods of lead generation and finding door knocking or cold calling a more reliable and effective source of lead generation.

Also remember many marketers wishing to stand out from the crowd make false promises that they can't keep and publish fake promotions to grab a lead, making it more difficult for people to determine with whom they can trust to do business with. Hence they end up signing up with people who approach them directly and offer face to face personalized service.

Even though this research indicates that many traditional methods are slow to blossom, time consuming, and costly, they should not be considered as ineffective. Again it really depends on your personality and personal preferences. Your strengths and evaluating what you do best is what should determine the direction you will take in this area of your business.

CHAPTER 10

HOW TO GENERATE REAL ESTATE LEADS

Until now we have talked a lot about lead generation encompassing the totality of the offline and online methods of generating leads. We have explored in detail various online methods of lead generation, their effectiveness and uses and similarly a lot about the offline lead generation techniques and the degree of their effectiveness. But remember that we don't live in an isolated world. We cannot simply segregate or separate offline methods and online methods of lead generation. In fact the idea behind exploring them separately was to help us identify which methods are the most effective and why, so that we are now ready to explore how we can develop an effective lead generation strategy while incorporating both the effective online and offline methods based on the marketer's skills and preferences.

An effective lead generation strategy would be the one that is well planned and pursues the most fruitful tactics that ensure the greatest success of your lead generation campaign based on the investor's unique situation.

Successful Lead Generation Campaign

- **Know yourself:**

  Before initializing any lead generation strategy it is especially important for every real estate marketer or investor to evaluate one's own self. One must identify and evaluate one's own limits and boundaries. Analyze your budgets. Evaluate what properties you hold? What types of properties you want to invest in? Who are your target buyers and sellers? Where to locate them?

For example if you deal in commercial plots or properties, your target market would be completely different from those of residential properties. Your lead search should be directed towards business people or small proprietors. Your marketing tactics would be entirely different. In fact your whole lead generation strategy depends on the type of properties and services you offer. Hence the first step of your lead generation process is your own self-evaluation. This is the reason why what works for others sometimes doesn't work for you as a real estate investor, you have your own limitations with respect to your budgets, resources, and types of properties you wish to deal with.

- **Know your customers:**

Once you know yourself and decide your target customers, now it is time to evaluate your prospective customers. Research extensively, to know their needs and preferences; identify their problems; evaluate their budgets and limitations. You can approach them by knocking doors in your neighborhood and asking them for information. Identify their sphere of influence, which is another critical factor in determining your lead generation strategy.

- **Identify current market trends:**

An industry appraisal is as important to a real estate investor as it is to any other business. It is crucial to keep an eye on the current market rates and prices. See what your competitors are offering. Gauge the changing economic factors that may affect the industry. As real estate investing often requires huge amounts of time & money, one wrong decision can quickly lead you to bankruptcy.

Before the recent onset of the recession many real estate investors believed that property prices could never actually fall sharply. They believed that the real estate market can only experience temporary and nominal price fluctuations but to their surprise the collapse of major investment hubs in the global market have hugely affected the real estate industry leaving hundreds of real estate investors losing their collective "shirts" and facing bankruptcy. Hence a prudent investor is never unaware of the market.

- **Update your statistics:**

  In order to reach effectively to your target leads it is essential for you to update your statistics. But what specifically do you need to update? You need to update the current demographics of your local markets. Identify the geographical block you want to target and then research about the number of families that live in that area and their average income. The average number of children in each family, the number of students, number of newly married couples, number of old pensioners, number of unemployed individuals living on state funds. Studying all these demographics will help you invest in the types of properties that will be in demand.

  Also many investors most of the time buy a property and then invest money into its rebuilding and furnishings. So if you know the earning capacity of your target leads only then can you make a prudent investment decision. In an average income neighborhood you will be considered a fool if you refurbish the properties with expensive state of the art facilities making it unaffordable for your target customers to buy them. Also in such situations you cannot invest too much money into your lead generation strategy or purposely keep your campaign cost low or prevent it from being low profile.

  You should perform this exercise when you enter a new market, or yearly for any market you are continuing to work, or when you become aware of any significant market changes or shifts in the areas you are working in or planning to enter.

Once you analyze all these factors in detail now you are ready enough to formulate an appropriate lead generation campaign including both offline and online modes of marketing. Here are the important steps:

- **Select your Lead generation approach:**

  Your research about your target market will be the guiding factor to help you determine your marketing approach. For example if your target market is business people or small investors locating a place for their shop or for their new office than your approach would be entirely different than if you were targeting single family home buyers. In order to generate such leads you have to get visibility in local newspapers, business magazines etc., you can also expand your networks by attending many seminars and property shows to reach your targets.

Giving out business cards to the local business people and meeting people informally in the local markets is an effective strategy. Consequently online marketing can help you identify your leads and an online appearance in spheres of influence and posting regularly on local business forums can help you generate your leads.

Alternatively if your target market is rich old pensioners, who after retirement wish to invest in the home of their dreams, your lead generation strategy would again be somewhat different. Older people prefer face to face meetings and personal visits. They have all the time in the world to sit and chat with you. They are more influenced by their friends and local circles in the town. Instead of focusing on online marketing your focus here should be personal marketing. Referrals are the most effective source of lead generation here. Visits to local doctors, local clubs, hospitals, churches or parks and developing friendly relationships with the locals are the best way to generate effective leads for this niche.

- **Expand your network:**

Irrespective of the lead generation strategy, one thing that every marketer should ensure is to expand their networking. Networking can be done online through joining forums, blogs, social media websites, posting articles on selected directories etc. At the same time the marketer should expand their networks offline as well; for example visiting home shows, attending local seminars and events, expanding networks through charity if possible, joining local clubs and supporting local sports etc. Networking is important to generate positive referrals and increase the number of your leads.

- **Lead follow-ups:**

  Lastly, and critically important, is the lead follow-up. Once you generate your leads it is quite possible that you may lose them if you don't follow them up quickly. We touched previously on this; the survey report sited earlier highlighted the link relating how weak or delayed lead follow-up can lead to you losing your prospects. In order to close a deal you need to add quick response boxes on your website. Disseminate all required information to your clients as soon as possible. Revisit them regularly to keep them on track. All this will help you increase your sales and ultimately raise your profits.

The above steps are very critical in ensuring an effective lead generation campaign. No matter what lead generation tactics you use or what your target market is, you must follow these steps to ensure success of your lead generation campaign and achieve your ultimate goal of success as a real estate investor.

CHAPTER 11

MISTAKES TO AVOID IN REAL ESTATE INVESTING

As many of you would agree *Real estate investing* is an extremely rewarding way to build your wealth. It is most commonly referred to as a gold mine . . . but if you don't use the right systems . . . it will ruin your business and put you into great difficulty. To keep the real estate investing business lucrative for you, you must follow certain principles. If you ignore them, you will not be able to achieve your investment goals. In this chapter we will explore some common mistakes that people often make in their real estate investing business and hence suffer failures. As a prudent investor you must avoid making these common mistakes.

Common Mistakes in Real Estate Investing

Listed below are some of the common reasons for failure in real estate investing:

- **Failure to determine budgets:** One of the most common reasons for failure is not keeping a tight grip on the budget. Remember a real estate business requires huge investments in the deals hence it is extremely important to regularly perform a cash flow analysis of your personal funds and determine a statement of financial position. A cash flow analysis is a must for you before entering into any kind of transaction. If you are not an expert you can even hire an accountant or financial planner to assist you before making investments.

- **Failure to conduct financial analysis of the property:** A very common reason for real estate investment failures is lack of expert financial analysis. Real estate investments are complex. The cost analysts of the projects you undertake are not simple. But many investors make decisions based on assumptions or their personal judgments. This is extremely unprofessional. Without detailed cost analysis on the project you won't know the value of the property or the cost of repairs or even what it costs you to buy and/or sell it, you can't just assume costs and execute a particular project. With tens or even hundreds of thousands of dollars at stake this could lead you to fall short of funds in the middle of a project and leave you to face a serious financial crisis. Remember once again that real estate investments are capital intensive and you need to manage your funds professionally. You need to plan your capital and identify sources to generate adequate capital, or else you will end up in a financial mess.

- **Inadequate Market Research:** Lack of proper market research is also a common real estate investing mistake. Don't make abrupt decisions. Take time and think before taking action. Gary MacDonald in one of his articles on common real estate investing mistakes mentions a short story of how he ended up over investing $55,000 in a couple of days without adequately analyzing the pros and cons of the investment[9], much to his chagrin. A mistake you certainly don't want to make. Hence beware of this real estate business mistake and make your decisions wisely i.e. invite property valuators and inspectors to assess properties before making investments.

- **Failure to locate effective business leads:** As I have mentioned throughout in this text that lead generation is extremely important for real estate investing success. But many people still don't realize that. Especially old investors, pre 9/11 time, still cherishing old times when they were used to hot prospects coming out of the woodwork of their offices and keeping them busy enough to make mountains of wealth. In fact the real estate scenario has now changed an awful lot in the last few years. Real estate lead generation doesn't work that way too much anymore. The industry norm has changed. Now investors have to strive hard to generate leads. The economic downturn has also hit the industry hard making it necessary for investors to hunt for effective leads.

- **Buying properties in poor locations:** Many inexperienced and naïve investors just get attracted by the property. They buy everything that looks good to them just like love at first sight. Sometimes just eye catching locations are enough to make them invest huge sums of money. Most of this type of investor faces failures in the long run. Location of the property must be accessed. You must analyze what locations will attract your target market. If you buy an apartment in a location that is far away from the local shopping centers and lacks infrastructure for transportation, you will have difficulty in finding buyers for that property. You should invest in locations where there is strong infrastructure including schools, community centers, shopping areas, transportation and parks, etc. So avoid buying in poor locations. This will help you generate high capital growth and build your wealth.

- **Lack of capability:** Another common reason for failure to meet your investment objectives is lack of capability in handling real estate projects. You need services of professionals from various fields in order to succeed as a real estate investor. As mentioned before you need financial experts to provide you with cash flow and financial analysis of the projects. You need expert property inspectors/analysis to help you evaluate market rates of the property. You need experienced architects and professional builders if you are undertaking any construction. You need economic experts to help you forecast market trends.
Many individual investors do hire property management companies but again if you end up signing a crappy one . . . . you may still wind up in a mess.

- **Ignoring the legal aspects:** Another major cause of failure is investing into legally tainted property. Sometimes you end up paying money to people who actually don't have the legal rights to the property. Be careful while investing in jointly owned properties. You may need the services of a real estate attorney to take care of the legal aspects. Also avoid investing in legally disputed properties. Remember you are incurring costs to generate funds for investments and disputed stakes take time to resolve and your money gets sucked up in such cases. So be a wise investor.

- **False promises:** Never make unrealistic or false promises while marketing your services. This will drive all your business away. Many marketers do use such techniques in order to grab at leads and these actions only serve to discredit and create distrust against all investors. This makes it more difficult for all of us to do business.

Hence all the above points signify that real estate investing is not as simple as it appears. In fact there is a lot to consider in real estate. You need to think smart. Think wisely about the costs, your budgets, the market trends, your lead generation, your position and location, and the legalities, before you enter into a transaction. Proper adherence to these steps means you have set the ball rolling on a smooth turf, and you can meet your investment goals, but neglecting critical steps is walking into danger. So be prudent.

CHAPTER 12

WHICH REAL ESTATE LEAD GENERATION METHOD IS RIGHT FOR YOU?

After exploring common real estate investing failures, we have once again highlighted the importance of effective lead generation, as the ineffective lead generation process is observed to be one of the most common reasons causing failures of real estate investing businesses. Therefore let's get back to the subject of lead generation again which is the core topic of this text.

Having discussed a number of lead generation methods, now it is time to evaluate which lead generation method(s) is appropriate for you. Before going further, one thing that is important to mention here is that there is no one right method. Something that works for someone else may not work for you. Hence there are many factors that affect the lead generation methods you need to utilize in your business. Additionally one also needs to understand that a single lead generation method or technique does not work on its own. In fact the real estate marketer needs to undertake a number of methods to run a successful lead generation campaign.

Now let's figure out a few factors that help you determine which lead generation method(s) is right for you:

- **The Budget:** As discussed previously real estate investing is a capital intensive business. Real estate investors need to setup and adhere to their budgets while conducting their business. Even to conduct a lead generation campaign it is important to evaluate your budgets. Select the best methods that fall within your budgets.

If you have little funds available you can opt for online methods of lead generation, for example using social sites like Facebook or Twitter for generate leads. If your pocket allows for it you might advertise on local TV channels or radio stations, if you can handle the huge costs.

- **The Target Market:** The selection of the right lead generation methods also depends on the market you are targeting. We have already explored this point in detail in one of our previous chapters. Hence evaluate your market first and then employ the appropriate lead generation techniques.

- **Comparing costs with benefits:** Cost benefit analysis is the tool that every wise marketer must use. Even if you have handsome budgets, you would not like to invest them in activities that generate lower benefits. So before investing in a lead generation method you must evaluate its benefits and compare it with the costs it incurs. (This topic will be discussed in detail in the next chapter)

- **Quality of your services:** You must be wandering just how your service quality can impact your decision over selecting the right lead generation method. Although your service quality has no direct effect on your choice of lead generation method it does have enormous impact on your overall lead generation campaign. As I mentioned earlier that referrals are the best way of generating effective leads, and referrals are in turn a product of outstanding customer service. Therefore if you provide the best service to your clients you will need to invest a bit in generating positive referrals—like referral incentive schemes which will be the best lead generation strategy in such cases.
  Hence, the more you know your market/industry and provide exceptional customer service, the less you will have to invest in lead generation. Good service itself can bring you hot leads right to your doorstep.

These are a few factors that will assist you in selecting the appropriate lead generation method. But once again I would like to highlight that every situation is different and what is good in one situation may not be as good in another different situation. So always evaluate your options before you make your decisions.

CHAPTER 13

ANALYZING THE COST TO BENEFIT RATIO OF A LEAD

Many marketers often implement the most expensive lead generation techniques in the hopes it will generate effective leads, providing they have adequate budgets. But this sometimes costs them more as compared to the benefits they obtain from generating those leads. What they don't evaluate is whether they will be able to get enough monetary benefits from the leads they obtain as compared to the costs they incurred. Hence cost to benefit analysis must be done before investing money into any lead generation method. Meaning costs per lead should be compared with the benefits you obtain from that lead.

In order to understand this in detail, let's go through a very simple example.

Cold calling as mentioned earlier is a very common and traditional method of generating leads in a real estate business. In order to make calls marketers usually buy calling lists from list generating companies. These lists are usually very expensive and contain the contact numbers of prospective leads. Once you obtain these lists you start calling people and marketing yourself to generate leads. But is this an effective tactic? What you are doing is actually calling a totally unknown person who doesn't know you and asking them to become your customer. Do you really think things work this way? Especially today, when people are fed up of such marketing calls and consider them junk or scams, (as mentioned earlier, this method requires a certain type of personality to be done successfully). The success ratio of such a strategy is very low. Even if you are lucky enough to generate a few leads the costs per lead you generate would be higher than the benefit you get from that lead. Remember that you cannot realize the benefit unless you enter into a transaction with your lead, which is to turn them into your client. This is what we call a cost benefit analysis, which is where you compare the costs with the benefits incurred.

Now let's come to the technical terms. In order to analyze the cost and benefits of the leads you generate focus on the following points:

- **Evaluate Return On Investment (ROI):** The profitability of any business investment can be determined by evaluating its returns. If your campaign generates positive ROI than it is wise to undertake that campaign. Also the higher the ROI the better is the campaign.

- **Cost per lead versus cost per sale:** Many marketers focus more on costs per lead than costs per sales. Remember that your ultimate objective is to generate sales not leads. What will you do with your leads if you cannot generate sales? You cannot realize your profits unless you generate sales. Hence real estate investors must determine the cost per sale to gauge the success of their lead generation campaign. At times some campaigns provide higher costs per lead but lower costs per sales. Hence costs per sale should be your key objective, which is still basically nothing more than return on your investment, (that is ROI).

- **Non-monetary factors affecting your ROI returns:** Before evaluating a campaign's success it should also be realized that many non-monetary factors can also affect the return on your investments. For example some campaigns that provided you higher return on sales and worked well for you may end in failure for some other investor. This can happen because of faster lead follow-up and better conversion techniques by one marketer promising them a higher return on their sales.

All these factors highlight that ROI should surely be gauged to evaluate the success of a lead generation campaign but at the same time the quality of services and lead follow-up procedures should also be evaluated to plan wise decisions for the future.

CHAPTER 14

LATEST LEAD GENERATION TECHNIQUES

- - - - - - - - - - - - - - - -

"THE SOCIAL NETWORKING SITES"

Over the years real estate investors have had to face certain challenges and hardships in finding prospective business leads. Many of the useful methods were often expensive, demanding huge investments. Then it was the internet that brought some relief for them. But today it has become even easier. All you have to do is to go on a popular social networking site and register yourself.

Social media sites are the most effective sources of generating business leads. Every day millions of internet users log-on to these social networking sites such as Facebook, Twitter, LinkedIn, etc. According to resent reports Facebook has become the most visited site on the web, more trafficked than even Google, making it one of the most popular sites for people to socialize and build relationships. Considering that Facebook has more than 500 million people registered who visit this web site daily for social networking, just imagine if you could reach them with only a few mouse clicks, how many leads could you generate at a minimum out of those 500 million people?

Apart from that the best thing is most of these sites are free of costs. You don't have to pay a single penny and get effective leads—marketing free of cost. What could be better?

Despite such huge benefits many real estate investors still don't know how they can get the benefit from these sites and generate an enormous number of effective leads for their business. In this chapter we will explore a few tips that will help you get the maximum out of these sites and generate effective leads.

- Register yourself on the Facebook web site and create a business page for your real estate business. It will serve as your landing page online. Also ensure to develop a title for your business page that is attractive and keyword based for example "lucrative real estate house", etc. or something like that.
- For the profile picture you can upload the logo of your company or business if you have one.
- You can produce details about your company and yourself on the profile page. In fact this will serve you as your website, if you don't have a business website.
- If you have a website, you can link these pages to your website, providing an opportunity to millions of Facebook users to visit your website once they view your profile.
- Once you have got a Facebook profile, you can use it for video marketing. All you have to do is to buy a good camera or even use your mobile to take pictures of the properties available for sale and post it there for free. You can also post videos on YouTube and provide links to them in your Facebook profile. Video marketing was never free before.
- You can join online groups, discussion forums or blogs and put your comments and post articles on them on a regular basis. This will help you to expand your networking and build your expertise, all free of cost.
- You can even search for prospective leads or groups (sphere of influence) by pasting appropriate search words in the search column and find prospective buyers.
- From time to time you can post any promotions or incentive you offer onto your wall to generate more leads.

Hence there can be infinite ways of generating leads on these social networking sites, with zero costs. In the next chapter we will explore one other modern form of lead generation—that is mobile marketing.

CHAPTER 15

STEPS TO GENERATING REAL ESTATE LEADS WITH MOBILE MARKETING

Mobile marketing is another of the latest and relatively inexpensive ways of lead generation. In this chapter we will explore various steps to generate effective leads through mobile marketing for your real estate business.

In today's era of the knowledge and information society if you ask a person what would be the two most important things without which you don't leave your home. They would surely say their credit card/money and their mobile. Cell phones are the popular modes of communication and have almost replaced landlines. In fact, with the advent of these latest technologies like smart phones, mobiles have nearly replaced many computers. Mobiles are considered as mini computers allowing you to surf the web, do research, and make contacts. With billions of people around the world using cell phones, mobile marketing provides you a massive opportunity to promote yourself and your products or services. In Japan and in various European countries companies offer consumers incentives to make their purchases using their mobile phones.

In the real estate business you can also put an effective mobile marketing plan into action. Now let's examine a few of the ways through which real estate investors can generate leads through mobile marketing:

- **SMS Text:** The most common method of lead generation is marketing through SMS text. Businesses round the world are marketing their services through SMS texts. You can do an internet search for businesses that provide these services and market listing information directly to cell phones.

Capitalizing on the power of mobile texting, you can include a direct call to action within your promotions through text messaging. For example you can provide a simple call to action from your websites, leaflets, sales letter etc., such as add a box note saying "Text trends to 1234 for getting the going market rates". This will provide you an opportunity to get in touch with interested prospects that can possibly become your future clients.

- **QR Codes:** QR codes provide you an opportunity to bring people to your websites directly from their cell phones. You can include the QR Code at the bottom of your flyers, sales letters, leaflets etc. that takes your prospective leads to a specific place on your website. QR codes can save your leads time from actually going to their computers and logging into your website. They can directly read into the QR code using their cell phone and visit your website.

- **Video Marketing through mobile phone:** With this latest technological advance, mobile phones can now be used as a medium for video marketing. For example devices like the I-phone have standard YouTube applications. You can use this opportunity to market your sales promotion and other videos.

- **Google Ad-Words:** Popular search engines like Google specifically allow you to approach a mobile user. For example you can create an Ad-Group that target users of I-phones. You can design short small-font messages to these users and generate leads for your business.

Hence, with the ever increasing number of cell phone users, you, as a real estate investor have the opportunity to massively grow your business by capitalizing on mobile marketing by using these above mentioned techniques.

CHAPTER 16

BENEFITS OF LOW COST LEAD GENERATION

As mentioned repeatedly throughout this text effective lead generation is the back bone of a real estate investment business. If you don't have effective leads you have no sales. Given its importance many real estate marketers believe that they should invest huge sums of money to implement an effective lead generation campaign. People usually think that the more money you put into your lead generation campaign the more benefits you can reap and the more leads you can generate. But this is not always the case. Expensive lead generation campaigns do not always guarantee success. There are a number of lead generation techniques that are not only outstandingly effective but are almost free of costs. In this chapter we will explore a few of them and the benefits thereto.

Low Cost Lead Generation Methods and Their Benefits

- Consider every person you meet or know as your lead: This sounds weird. Isn't it? I personally thought this too. But this technique actually works. Betty Ziegler in one of her articles on *low cost lead generation in the real estate industry* highlights that this technique exclusively suits the real estate business. She maintains that by categorizing every person you know as your potential lead and start providing them some value, they would ultimately be turned into your client. Value can be in terms of greeting, in terms of meeting them and talking to them, value in terms of listening to their problems, exchanging e-mails and finally market your business. The core concept lies in initiating contacts and building relationships with people. Once you do that they will surely become your clients as people in the real estate market usually prefer one to one relationships.[10]

This philosophy described by Betty Zeigler was more or less ascertained from a study conducted by the National Association of Realtors® (NAR). After a survey of a group of real estate agents the study concluded that more than sixty percent of buyers/sellers usually choose the first real estate agent they come in contact with[11]. The same would be true for an investor seeking customers. Hence this signifies that if you want to make an effective lead all you need to do is to initiate contact. Talk to them, the more you know your leads and provide exceptional customer service, the less you will have to invest in lead generation.

- **Provide exceptional customer service:** Another effective and low cost lead generation technique is providing quality service to your present clients. But what does this have to do with generating leads. Again the answer is simple; *satisfied customers can bring you hot leads right to your doorstep* as mentioned earlier through positive referrals. You can also write an *'Endorsement Letter'* for your client, give it to them and ask them if they would be comfortable sending it to their neighbors. You can ask your client to sign this letter for credibility. This is a tested and proven strategy that can generate future leads, almost free of costs.

Now let's consider the benefits:

Benefits of Low Cost Lead Generation Methods

The benefits of these strategies are enormous. Here is the list:

- These are almost free techniques.
- These techniques provide you quality leads.
- Provide high lead to sale conversion ratio.
- Build-up credibility in the industry.
- You don't need to invest too much into closing a transaction.
- Provides high return on investment (ROI)

CHAPTER 17

METHODS TO ACTIVATE REAL ESTATE LEADS GENERATION

We have talked a lot about lead generation methods. We will not talk about them directly in this chapter. So what's new that I am going to cover? Any guesses??????!!!!!!!!!!!!!!

In this chapter, I am going to discuss the only technique that keeps lead generation active and alive and that is what we all know as *"Networking"*.

We all know that lead generation is the life blood of any business but what keeps this life blood running or flowing is the *"Networking"*. It is essential for every real estate marketer to understand that lead generation is an ongoing process. There is no ending point or full stop. If you end this process your business is going to be dead very soon. And networking is the only way to keep the process of lead generation activated.

In simple words networking is nothing but expanding your circle, enhancing your contacts and getting visible in the market. There are a number of ways of expanding your networks. Continue reading to find out a few:

Techniques to Expand Networks

- **Attract A Sphere of Influence:** You need to identify the sphere of influence of your target market. Then try attracting them by sending out an introductory letter telling them about you and your business. Follow-up with them at regular intervals and once you build your rapport seek referrals from them.

- **Expand Offline Circles:** You should actively grow your contacts by getting in touch with builders and developers, architecture firms, local mortgage brokers, housing contractors, real estate attorneys and even bankers or loan officers. By putting your name on their lists, you can raise your chances of them forwarding it on to their clients.

- **Socialize offline:** Socializing with people provides you an opportunity not only to know them but also to tell them about yourself. A real estate marketer must take every opportunity to talk and meet people within their locality. You should participate in local events, home fairs, and shows. You can also organize or participate in organizing events in community clubs like community sports, health shows, Go Green campaigns, etc. Other attractive places for socializing are local doctors, churches, hair salons, and even corner shops. Yes, all these places are actually venues of local gatherings where people meet and share their problems and if someone recommends you at such gatherings, trust me, you will get hot leads already high to sign up a sale with you.

- **Join online Forums and Blogs:** if you want to look more professional, join related forums online and try to post regularly on them to build your credibility and show your expertise.

- **Social Networking sites:** These provide you an opportunity to socialize with your prospects online and expand your contacts globally with a couple of mouse clicks.

- **Get in the News:** Getting into the news here doesn't mean advertising or marketing your business. It is indeed the other way around. It means writing articles in the news media. This requires professionalism and consistency, but it can do wonders for your business. Local newspapers and magazines are the best place to start. You can speak or write on various issues like sharing real estate stories, industry highlights, etc. By getting visible on media, you can generate future leads.

Hence all of the above techniques can actually help you enhance your network and bring business for you in the long run.

CHAPTER 18

TAKING ANY LEAD GENERATION METHOD AND MAKE IT WORK FOR YOU

So far so good! If you are serious about real estate investing, I can tell you for sure that you must have found so much useful information in this book. We have discussed a lot about real estate marketing and lead generation and explored so many useful techniques, tips, and methods to help boost your real estate lead generation, which can certainly bring you fortunes and raise your bottom line. So what are you thinking about? Pack your bags and off you go . . . . !!!

WAIT !!!!!!!!!!!!!!!!!!!!!!!!!!

Before wrapping up this text I would like to ask you a question. By now most of you must have selected one or more methods you think are the most useful for your business and you will definitely try to use them to generate leads. But can you tell me;

How?

What course of action will you take?

Do you have an action plan?

If not, don't worry, I would never lead you astray. The next few paragraphs will get you ready to go into the market and start your action plan in the real world.

Steps To Put Your Lead Generation Method into Action

There are many different methods of generating real estate leads. But the success of your lead generation campaign does not only depend on the efficacy of the method but also on the way you put these methods into action in the real world. In order to explore how you do actually make any of these lead generation methods work for you in a real business setting, you must follow the below mentioned steps:

- **Choose the best method (s):** Picking out the best method seems an easy task, but it is actually not. Investors should realize that the success of their business lies in these lead generation methods. If you take the first step in the wrong direction and pick an ineffective method, you will descend along the wrong path. So think vigorously and evaluate all possibilities.

  It is also equally possible that you might have to pick out a number of methods to run at the same time as a whole lead generation campaign. Just take the example of marketing or promotion campaigns of various familiar companies we see every day, where they market their product or promotional campaign through using a multichannel approach, including print media, bill boards, TV, Radio, and even the internet all at the same time. The same can happen in your lead generation campaign where you may need to put a number of lead generation methods into action simultaneously to ensure success. Whatever is the case, pick your strategy wisely.

- **Identify the key areas and prioritize your work:** Setting priorities is essential for any action plan. Identify the key areas of action and then prioritize them. This will help you to smoothly follow the action plan and save you time. For example if you want to expand your networking through participating in various professional forums, you must first be on your toes and research the related information extensively to be discussed in these forums, before joining these groups. Otherwise you will lose your credibility.

- **Develop back-up plans:** Most marketers often ignore back-up plans or they might be extraordinarily optimistic. Remember that in the real world many unexpected things can happen which are outside your control. So always prepare back-up plans, this will save you time. If you don't do that you might lose your leads to your competitors.

- **Visualize and fill in the gaps:** Pay attention. Once you put the plan into action you might visualize something lacking or see gaps. Stop right away and try to fill in the gap. Remember this is the initial stage; rectify yourself immediately to follow the right track. So keep your eyes and ear open and evaluate every step as you move ahead.

- **Feedback:** You must evaluate every step of the process and give feedback to yourself. Jot down what worked and what didn't. This will help you improve your performance in the future.

Hence these simple steps if taken before putting a lead generation campaign into full action can optimize the success of that lead generation campaign by helping you generate sales and earn more profits.

CHAPTER 19

SECRETS OF SUCCESSFUL
LEAD GENERATION

Now it's time to reveal some comprehensive secrets to successful lead generation. Are we talking about something out of the box? Some extra magic!?

Throughout this book we have explored in detail the fundamentals of lead generation in a real estate investing business. First, we highlighted the importance of lead generation in a real estate investing business. Then we discussed about the various methods, techniques and ways through which effective leads can be generated online. We have also explored processes that will help us move up the success ladder. Hence we explored nothing but the most effective tactics of lead generation in a real estate business.

Now if I were asked to produce a synopsis of this text and write a short paper on the successful generation of leads, the whole idea explored in this text can be condensed into the last few following paragraphs, which could be titled as: ***The Secrets of Successful Lead Generation***. The crux of this whole book in fact lies in these paragraphs revealing the crucial secrets of success in a real estate investing business.

Secrets of Successful Lead Generation

Before revealing the secrets let's conduct a simple little exercise by answering the following questions one by one:

- What are effective leads? *The leads that can possibility be converted into sales.*

- What type of leads can be converted into sales easily? *The ones, who are satisfied about you and your services!*
- When do leads get satisfied? *When they value you and find you trustworthy.*
- How can you bring value and build trust? *By providing quality service to the ones who are interested in your business!*
- How do you get them interested in your services? *By being visible in the market and marketing yourself in a way that brings your leads towards your business.*

Most of you reading this must be wandering why I am asking these questions? This may seem silly. But this is a brainstorming exercise. The whole idea behind this exercise is to help us identify the process by which we can define the underlying secrets around which the success of the lead generation methods revolves, which I will now reveal.

Bring Leads to Your Doorstep

The success of any lead generation method can somewhat be assured when your prospects come to your business without direct or continuous effort from you. But how can you make this possible? Or in other words how can you make people want to contact you? Especially in this highly competitive real estate market where your target leads are daily exposed to hundreds of marketers striving hard to grab their attention.

I am sure by now most of you would have thought of a number of techniques or methods that can work to generate interest in your leads and trigger them to contact you. I am pleased with your progress in this endeavor. My interest now is in revealing the 3 basic secrets that underline and define each and every one of these methods, the secrets are:

- **Be Visible:** Be visible to let people realize that you do exist in the industry. How can they contact you if they don't even know that you exist? So be visible everywhere online as well as offline. We have explored many ways through which you can expand your contacts and develop referrals for your business. The more visible you are, the greater the chances that your leads will come to you.

- **Be valuable:** The most successful marketers today in the real estate industry are the ones who understand the concept of perceived value. In order to generate positive leads, visibility is not enough. As a real estate investor you must do your best to increase your perceived value, which is your value in the eyes of your clients. For this you have to show that you are an expert in the field and can provide ultimate value to your customers.

- **Be trustworthy:** Last but not least. You also need to develop trust in the eyes of the customers. This can be done by providing exceptional, high quality services and by fulfilling your promises etc. Always remember to never make false promises to attract your leads.

Hence finally we can summarize that the whole idea of successful lead generation processes revolve around these basic secrets. Being visible, Being valuable, Being trustworthy, and if you ensure this, it will help you generate attractive leads, help you make your real estate business flourish and will make your real estate lead generation efforts work in short order to get you started right away as well as in the long run which ensures the prosperity of you and your business.

MORE PUBLICATIONS

<u>REPORTS</u>

SURVIVED THE FINANCIAL MELTDOWN?

UNDERSTANDING SHORT SELLING: A COMPLETE GUIDE!

SELLER FINANCING: AND OTHER CREATIVE FINANCING TECHNIQUES

<u>WEEKLY NEWSLETTER</u> SIGN-UP AT   http://www.newworldreinvesting.com/

READ & COMMENT ON OUR BLOG   http://newworldreinvesting.wordpress.com/

Like Us on Facebook   http://www.facebook.com/pages/New-World-Real-Estate-Investing/128991903916875?ref=hl

FOLLOW US ON TWITTER   http://twitter.com/newworldreinvesting

REFERENCES

1   http://www.investopedia.com/university/real_estate/real_estate1.asp#axzz1n0fcGbW1

2   http://www.baylor.edu/business/kellercenter/index.php?id=55738

3   http://www.baylor.edu/business/kellercenter/index.php?id=55741

4   http://www.theregister.co.uk/2004/08/09/online_as_spend/

5   http://blog.nielsen.com/nielsenwire/global/social-networking-new-global-footprint/

6   http://mashable.com/2010/03/01/social-networks-source-news

7   http://www.brainyquote.com/quotes/quotes/s/samueljohn137084.html

8   http://www.baylor.edu/business/kellercenter/index.php?id=55741

9   http://ezinearticles.com/?Four-of-the-Most-Costly-Mistakes-Residential-Property-Investors-Make-and-How-to-Avoid-Them&id=2748473

10 http://ezinearticles.com/?Low-Cost-Lead-Generation-Brings-Exclusive-Real-Estate-Leads&id=3070974

11 http://ezinearticles.com/?Which-Real-Estate-Lead-Generation-Method-Is-Right-For-You?&id=5465378

www.ingramcontent.com/pod-product-compliance
Lightning Source LLC
Chambersburg PA
CBHW021902170526
45157CB00005B/1938